PETER McDONOUGH SR.

Particles
Of Truth
In Fractured
Sunlight

AuthorHouse™
1663 Liberty Drive
Bloomington, IN 47403
www.authorhouse.com
Phone: 833-262-8899

This book is printed on acid-free paper.

ISBN: 978-1-6655-3277-8 (sc)
ISBN: 978-1-6655-3278-5 (hc)
ISBN: 978-1-6655-3276-1 (e)

Library of Congress Control Number: 2021914803

Print information available on the last page.

Published by AuthorHouse 09/24/2021

authorHOUSE®

I would like to dedicate this book to my wife and love of my life Jaybee Del Prado McDonough. I am happy to spend my life with you. Some people have better half's - you arc and always will be my better four fifths.

I would also like to recognize my mother Mary McDonough. All those books you read to me as a child are remembered and both the books and the memories of the time spent are cherished.

CONTENTS

PARTICLES OF TRUTH

There is a fractured light that shines,

Through a plain glass window pane,

It reminds me of the mirrors of my youth.

When I was young and strong,

My future undecided,

I was gazing at the world and seeking truth.

MOONLIGHT

A folk song -

Well, you can look at the moonlight,

You can believe in second sight,

You can believe in what you want to believe,

But you know that, you still grow older tonight,

We can sit neath the moonlight,

We can get lost in each other's eyes,

We can talk about what is wrong and what is right,

But we still grow older tonight.

When I was a young man,

I had a young man's dreams,

And I held on to those dreams,

Like a priest holds on to belief,

Then I met a young girl,

She had a young girl's dreams,

All that she really needed,

Was a young man she could believe,

Well you can look at the moonlight,

You can believe in second sight,

You can believe in what you want to believe,

But you know that, you still grow older tonight,

We can sit neath the moonlight,

We can get lost in each other's eyes,

We can talk about what is wrong and what is right,

But we still grow older tonight.

When I was a young boy,

I had a friend who was dear to me,

And he used to tell me,

What good friends we'd always be,

Now that I am older,

I sometimes say, "where could my friends be?"

You know sometimes they can be hard to find,

When you find your're most in need.

Well you can look at the moonlight,

You can believe in second sight,

You can believe in what you want to believe,

But you know that, you still grow older tonight,

We can sit neath the moonlight,

We can get lost in each other's eyes,

We can talk about what is wrong and what is right,

But we still grow older tonight,

But we still grow older tonight,

But we still grow older tonight.

CHAPTER THREE

DEADICATED

Have you dared ever notice,

The silence that approaches,

With the coming of the night,

As we spread our frail wings,

Drop all worldly things,

And soar off with soft flight,

Can you possibly imagine,

What would happen,

If we did not come home tonight,

But left our frail lives,

So far behind,

And momentarily died?

CHAPTER FOUR

WITHIN OR WITHOUT

The ghost that's within goes without sometimes,

Like the thought inside of one's head not let out,

Like the word or the words left unsaid bout the thought,

That thou screaming to go past the lips won't get out,

If let go it could alter the consciousness stream that flows,

Through the twisted world order that unseen still exists,

To keep peace or at least the image of calm,

Where outside one displays a dull tranquil daze

And inside an entire world war is ablaze,

Where one has flipped script on the thought in one's head,

Where imprisoned it remains safely unsaid,

Like a ghost kept within that's without,

Like a spirit that's hungry but unfed.

CHAPTER FIVE

EASTERN SHORE

I sit beneath low clouds there blowing,

Just above the taller trees,

Blown way fast by warm fall winds,

Blown to places I can't see,

Over city streets criss crossing,

Past power line infinity,

Past cornfields swaying without breaking,

Eastern shore corn on the bay,

Through the tree lines grown to save,

The fields from winds that blow this way,

Over piers and stone wall breakers,

Past bouncing buoys out to sea,

My clouds are gone now,

All dispersed,

Till spring rains bring them back to me.

CHAPTER SIX

TRAVEL

Step by step I travel,

Though it's measured different ways,

Sometimes it feels I've moved but yards,

And my destination is far away,

One foot falls as up one rises,

Some people's feet pass the other way,

I do not see their faces,

Destinations do not let them stay,

Some who've passed leave tracks I follow,

Some of my steps left tracks too,

My own it seems I seldom see them,

From my forward facing point of view,

On and on my travels take me,

This way that, but not back again,

It's best I think not where I'm going,

It's best I think not where I've been.

CHAPTER SEVEN

PG COUNTY
NOCTURNAL BLUES

Well...

I've chased ghosts,

In the early morning moonlight,

With dark souled companions,

Whose minds were not quite right,

The only thing they could do right,

Was lead a young man wrong,

The only thing they cared a bit about,

Was the act of carrying on.

I've chased ghosts,

In the early morning moonlight,

Chased em to ground level windows,

In the older run down part of town,

At the hour when the blinds have eyes,

But still hear more than they see,

Down lonely crisscrossed streets,

Where no good folk are found.

I've chased ghosts,

In the early morning moonlight,

My friends have now departed,

With the ghosts I cannot catch or see,

Some remain on skeleton frames,

With sunken eyes that stare through me,

A ghost don't owe a soul to find,

What a soul's got no business looking for,

An apparition's best disguise,

Is a late night mirror through an open door.

CHAPTER EIGHT

EYESIGHT IN NEAR DARK

She puts flirting before sleeping,

On her to do list before bed,

She smiles wryly in her knowledge,

That she can read what's in my head,

She sees reflections of herself,

In my blue eyes by candlelight,

While I am lost within her brown eyes,

Just as if I'd shut mine tight,

She reads volumes at a glance,

In her keen sight reads my mind,

I know she knows how much I love her,

Before I tell her from time to time.

CHAPTER NINE

WAITING FOR YOU

Flamenco Ballad for Jaybee 1994

"Why am I, wasting my time,

Loosing my mind, waiting for you,

How can I, capture you to my side,

Call you to be my bride,

Call you to me

Love won't let me, let you go,

You look so lost, lost and alone,

Love is full, full of fears,

Love will lead you, lead you to tears,

Why am I, wasting my time,

Loosing my mind, waiting for you,

How can I, capture you to my side,

Call you to be my bride,

Call you to me....

I want to take you, take you home,

You look so lost, lost and alone,

I want to make it, make it known,

I want to make you, make you my own,

Why am I, wasting my time,

Loosing my mind, waiting for you,

How can I, capture you to my side,

Call you to be my bride,

Call you to me...."

Repeat to fade...

CHAPTER TEN

SPENDING TIME

What if it's all just - a waste of time?

You sell plastic cups and I sell butchers twine,

Where would the world be - without the sales we make each time?

Where would our loves be without the money we leave behind?

Would somebody notice - If we stole away?

I have an old car and you have the maps you've saved,

What would the world say if we checked out and left?

Where would we go if we didn't feed off our success?

We wake up each morning and sell them on their need,

The higher the margins = the more that we succeed,

Sometimes it's confusing, sometimes it's hard to see,

If I'm selling these things or if I'm selling me,

What if it's all just a waste of time?

I wait for my shift to end, I watch the clock make time,

A second approaches as another is left behind,

Where would my mind be without knowledge of this kind?

Where would our loves be without the money we leave behind?

What if we up and wandered away?

I've got some change for gas,

You've got the maps you saved,

Would somebody notice,

If we called out each day?

Would anyone care that we had simply slipped away,

What if it's all just a waste of time?

You sell lemon juice and I sell fresh limes,

Where would the world be without the drinks they make each time?

Where would our loves be without the money we leave behind?

What if it's all just a waste of time?

What if it turns out...

it's all just nickels and dimes.

CHAPTER ELEVEN

SPACE IS A DOORWAY

There is a sunlight crack in the screen door,

It hasn't held darkness since you left me,

Now the light flows through the door you split wide,

And spills to the counter and kitchen floor,

The joy of silence fills the void of you,

I wade through thoughts like a child in water,

Thoughts of my own I do not need to share,

I'm not required to think as you do,

Worry me some for the winter draws near,

Cold enters as easily as the light,

A fear of alone like frost fills my mind,

Joy for you leaving or joy for you here

Blue moonlight fills cracks where the sunlight came,

And me some dust in the light I remain.

ENTER SPACE

As I enter space I face,

All things in their proper place,

No good no bad, not one small trace,

Nothing.

As I leave behind time I find,

An absence of thought within my mind,

A crack through which there no light shines,

A tranquility of a different kind,

Nothing.

TELEPHONE BLUES

It's the fifth ring of the phone that really kills me,

I die completely inside shortly after the fourth,

If someone truly loves you they answer it quick you know,

Like they've an impatience in life to experience conversation with you,

Like they can't get enough so they want to experience it sooner,

By the fifth ring you know they haven't got the time

or the inclination to be bothered,

They've more pressing matters at hand that must be attended to first,

They can hear an alarm that your sounding five times

but they have to do other things first,

Each ring feels like an eternity of absence,

Each ring feels alone.

CHAPTER FOURTEEN

TAKING STOCK

A pause on a passionless plateau of coexistence,

A moment to stop and reflect upon a more meaningful time,

An agonizing prospect just to think of what was,

A glimmer though dimming of a moment more kind.

An uninviting place we haven't been to before.

A hope to pass through this gateway of loss,

A desire to come through on the right side of us,

A dream that we hold on regardless of cost.

CHAPTER FIFTEEN

A PERCOCET'S BLUES

Nothing could ever be so lonely as the last Percocet in a tan pill bottle,

It has a loneliness that speaks of waking up alone after a midnight orgy,

A desperation of calling a phone with no answering machine,

while knowing the residents are gone,

There's no sound less fulfilling than the rattle that one pill makes,

in an otherwise empty jar,

Like the dingdong sound of the idiot light;

when the gas is almost gone in your car,

Like the last car left in a parking lot,

Like the last note played on a guitar.

Nothing could be of less purpose,

Than to know that your job was to fix how one feels,

and to know one will hurt - more than one heals.

CHAPTER SIXTEEN

OPPRESSIVE FEELING

A Folk Melody

There's a pretty oppressive feeling and it's hanging over me,

Like the lightning on the treetops or a gale upon the seas,

And it's sent from you to me my love like a message on the breeze,

And it says you won't becoming round no more,

And that tells me you don't love me any more.

I've spent my time down deep inside soul searching as they say,

Looking for a path that's clear or easy anyways,

In all my time I've yet to find a woman who would stay,

I guess it's time I turn my head and slowly fade away,

I guess sometimes the more we try the more we fade away,

I will still be sitting here until the end of day,

Wondering what's become of you, oh have you gone away,

Instrumental....

There's a pretty good light by which I see attribute that to past,

Like sad dreams or just bad memories which fade but never pass,

I've traveled different roads and I have strayed from path to path,

But you were one with whom I thought the feelings would still last,

You were one with whom I thought my dreams would come at last,

And I will still be sitting here until the day has passed,

Wondering what's become of you and why we did not last."

CHAPTER SEVENTEEN

LOOK YOU AT ME

1990

Look you at me and see the world we know is turning,

Look you at me and see I long for a returning,

To the very simple lives worth living,

Satisfy my soul with giving,

All of myself to you freely,

Can't you see?

Look how the snow outside falls in its soft flurry,

Look how the men all round bustle fuss and hurry,

It's like some pressure valve or safety net,

They fix what needs no fixing yet,

And wipe away all clarity in thoughtless form.

Look how the wind blows round in its rampant furry,

There there my hats blown off,

Come on quick now hurry,

It's like we have no time to wonder why,

Now we must but do then die,

And that is what I fear the most,

Will life pass by?

Look how my arms stretch wide when I first awaken,

My muscles flex so strong but I do not feel strengthened,

It's like some leprosy or bad disease,

It saps at all that I believe,

Until I'm not sure which is which,

Or right from wrong,

Look how our world grows large when we are enlightened,

Look how our minds expand when no longer frightened,

It's like we have to see - to believe,

Where we've been and where we'll be,

Until such time that we might find,

Familiar ground.

CHAPTER EIGHTEEN

HOME

1994

I want to go home,

To places I'm familiar with,

Places that I have been,

Where no one else goes,

I want to see things,

Seen through my adjusted eyes,

See straight through their clever disguise,

Things I never see,

I want to hear sounds,

Sounds that I no longer hear,

By following a road that's clean and clear,

Following you,

(Refrain)

And if you should stay,

Should I go,

What if I get lost on my way,

To your home,

Will you wait for me,

Wait till I can see,

A path that's followed easily

To your door,

Instrumental....

(Refrain)

And if you should stay,

Should I go,

What if I get lost on my way,

To your home,

Will you wait for me,

Wait till I can see,

A path that's followed easily

To your door,

I want to grow old,

Just like my papa did,

And ten papa's before him did,

I want to die old,

I want to give back,

To all those who gave to me,

A sense of security,

A sense of love,

(Refrain)

And if you should stay,

Should I go,

What if I get lost on my way,

To your home,

Will you wait for me,

Wait till I can see,

A path that's followed easily,

To your door,

A path that's followed easily,

To your door,

A path that's followed easily,

To your door.

CHAPTER NINETEEN

SUNSET EMPIRE

We had Cadillac dreams,

Shared with our coach bag queens,

Dime store budgets with finance options,

We carried the weight of our perpetual myth,

We were temporarily displaced millionaires.

We drank nine dollar coffees,

They were pumpkin and spice,

We had special sauce stains on our shirts.

We firmly believed - we were on our way up,

But when you purchase your pain it still hurts.

We had diesel stack trucks display patriot prayers,

As they parked at their corporate bank homes.

End time world watchers passed watchtower leaflets,

They wanted ten percent of what we did not own.

We held up our previous poet's,

Like gas mask tributes in the trenches of our despair,

Like pillbox sparrows unaware of the loss,

Like the living passing dead man's.graves,

Swearing that what was given was not in vain.

The experiment ended and democracy lost

Not from force or arms under battlefield flags,

When this empire crumbled it was quiet and slow,

It was purchased,

It was bought,

It was sold.

CHAPTER TWENTY

THE KING OF A CRUMBLING CASTLE

I was once the ruler of this land

The man who earned more, the man who did more, he through which all things provided came,

Then I stopped racing towards the sun

The man who stood still, the man who rested, he who watched the world race by,

Then I could not remember why I moved

The man who forgot, the man confused, he who lost purpose in said direction.

Then I saw those I loved were still moving

The man who reached out, the man who sought out, he who wanted to carry on

CHAPTER TWENTY-ONE

THE CAR RIDE

She doesn't care about politics,

Or the wars sometimes fought in the front seat of the car

She counts telephone poles and draws faces,

Her finger tips off the lid,

As she paints her way out of their jar.

No internet news or conflicting world views,

Just a canvas of glass and her hands,

She can walk through the streets of their anger,

As if in some far away land.

CHAPTER TWENTY-TWO

BLOWN OUT

I'm not really sure where I am going,

I seem to be lost on my way,

Do you know where you're going,

Seems like such a sunny day,

I need to know you believe in me,

I need to know it more than anything you can conceive,

Without knowledge of my destiny you see,

Seems the clouds will roll my way,

Seems the clouds will roll my way,

Seems the clouds will roll my way,

Seems the clouds will roll my way,

"Instrumental"

I've got a hand and I have got a glove that fits,

I've got a code of ethics to describe the way I live,

Will you be here when the sun don't shine,

Or will you be gone on your way,

Will you be gone on your way,

Will you be gone on your way,

Will you be gone on your way,

"instrumental"

Ten men stand for things they don't believe,

One man stands for something only he can see,

If you hold a candle to the wind,

Will the flame always blow out,

Will the flame always blow out,

Will the flame always blow out,

Will the flame always blow out.

CHAPTER TWENTY-THREE

SHE'S PERFECTION

She's that pretty girl wandering around aimlessly at every accident scene,

Her beauty enhanced ten fold by the chaos and carnage that surrounds her,

She's a screen covering the bloodiest parts,

From the ever searching gap mouthed gawkers passing by,

As they look her way instead.

She is perfect.

She's a pleasant commercial,

For a non profit endeavor to make the world a better place,

During a really shitty Re-run,

She's not actually selling anything or pushing things we don't need,

She fulfills her prophecy of a better world every minute she exists in it,

She's perfect.

She's the empty park and ride on a Sunday morning at the edge of town,

You can stop and rest in her open space and watch the world rush by,

It's a large enough space to scream your rage,

And she won't divulge your secrets,

to any of the hurried souls flitting about outside,

She's perfect.

CHAPTER TWENTY-FOUR

BRICK BY BRICK

(Three bar blues"

Well... brick by brick we build up heah and stone by stone we tear down,

Brick by brick we build up heah and stone by stone we tear down,

Tear down...

Mama mama, what'd you do with your life,

Me I'm trying to live mine right,

Goes by too quick and passes from sight,

Beneath encroaching city lights,

Well... brick by brick we build up heah and stone by stone we tear down,

Brick by brick we build up heah and stone by stone we tear down,

Tear down...

Mama mama, where'd you go?

You left walking between the corn rows,

Well you plant your seeds based on what you know,

But who will you feed now that we all grown?

Well... brick by brick we build up heah and stone by stone we tear down,

Brick by brick we build up heah and stone by stone we tear down,

Tear down...

Mama mama, where you been?

You've been walking the graveyard again,

Walk it with reverence, walk it real slow,

They gave us their lives and we gave them all stones.

Well... brick by brick we build up heah and stone by stone we tear down,

Brick by brick we build up heah and stone by stone we tear down,

Tear down... tear down... tear down.... tear down....

CHAPTER TWENTY-FIVE

THE THRONE

I would like to rule the world,

No - I dont think I would,

Perhaps someday I could,

But only if I had the time to waste.

I would like to sing a song,

With very simple music and very simple words,

Yet to complex to understand,

I would like to taste some fruit,

The same old fruit but in a different way,

I would like to appreciate it.

I wouldn't mind loosing my mind,

But if I concluded it was already lost,

I suppose I would have to find it first.

CHAPTER TWENTY-SIX

NO PLACE TO GO

Dirty Blues

Well....

I ain't got no place to go,

Except down to the sea,

And if you ain't got no place to go,

Why don't you come down with me,

And Suzy ain't got no place to go,

Except down to the sea with me,

And when we get there you know it about,

She gonna be down with me,

Instrumental...

Well...

All around this crazy town,

The people jump round and round round,

Midnight comes and rolls around,

And then we find out who's down, down,

Wish upon a falling star,

Wish you were not who you are,

Wish you had some cash to spend,

Then wonder where it went,

Instrumental...

Well...

Here's to all the crazy people,

Here's to all the lunatics,

Here's to all the late night freaks,

Who wonder where it went.

CHAPTER TWENTY-SEVEN

OUR HOME

A red brick house on a corner lot,

A red brick house on a hill,

All my life spent in one spot,

All my life standing still,

A brick house on a hill,

Built by a grandfather you never met,

One yard away from your grandma's house,

Whom You love dearly,

Us a family of five living on our corner lot,

With firewood piled high,

And a great Dane roaming the yard,

Sometimes the wind makes the front door moan,

Like a tired tugboat signaling home,

The driveway winds around the house,

Stretching to touch both streets,

It confuses the pizza delivery man,

When we order our food to eat.

CHAPTER TWENTY-EIGHT

LADY LAURA

Lady Laura took one last look

at her lover boarding ship,

Which would bear him to the sea which bore no feelings for his trip.

Lady Laura walked the shoreline to the last good rocky knoll,

She stood amongst a small group waving, he did not see and would not know.

The wind picked up, the ship set sail, the crowd dispersed for home,

Lady Laura wrapped her shawl around her and she remained to watch it go.

Lady Laura walked the cobbled streets of the village by the shore,

Past the baker and the dress maker, down empty streets she'd walked before.

She hung her shawl and coat,

As she walked inside the door,

And she climbed - her body tired, to her bedroom up the stairs,

Where she combed out all the tangles that the sea had made her hair,

Lady Laura lit the candle in the window facing shore,

And like so many nights before,

Lady Laura slept alone.

CHAPTER TWENTY-NINE

SALES DAY

Plastic molded figurines,

Who live in cardboard houses,

Selling each other prototype concepts of plans for a profit filled future,

Items that the algorithms told them to love,

A love based on the answers they gave to studies that were once conducted in market research department cubicles,

As each sales day comes,

They rise to the challenge,

Wearing plastic smiles given to them by plastic positivity counselors,

who work the circuit,

trading enlightened happiness knowledge for cash,

Armed with this knowledge and a healthy dose of senseless circle speak,

They close like tigers on the scent of inequity perception easily recognized by the blank, tired, lifeless expressions on each of the buyer's faces.

CHAPTER THIRTY

"The Diligent Ones"

We are the sons and daughters of the diligent ones,

The one's who worked so long and hard for this land we play upon,

The one's who sacrificed their lives, giving free of spirit, free from ties,

Longer youths and safer lives,

With which we run and play.

Play on you children of the night,

Dance and sing to your hearts delight,

Like a majestic bird lost in flight,

Exercising it's freedom,

For Freedoms that remain untested,

are earthbound birds that will not fly.

CHAPTER THIRTY-ONE

THE HEALING

I'll let the thread untangle between us.

I'll untie the knots and let my end go.

Free from the anguish this twisted line causes,

Free from the anger it's caused us to know.

I'll sweep from the floor the lies that were spoken.

I'll broom away misunderstandings - half truths.

Clean will be thoughts I'll have moving forward,

Clean as a fresh mopped, wood floor room.

I'll throw away broken pieces now shattered,

Of treasured times shared but not not cared for that broke.

If a vessel is cracked it no longer holds water,

I will dispose of what's held without use.

CHAPTER THIRTY-TWO

SOME SUMMER SONGS

(A blues song)

Some summer songs are sung while sitting

In the shade of an old oak tree,

Some summer songs go all night long to a youth who live carefree,

Sometimes sitting here I begin thinking bout all I used to be,

And though I have not sat here long,

I'm glad you're sitting with me.

Sunny time funny time laughing with my buddies while we share a joke or two,

Start walking round talking about sweet little ventures and all we used to do,

When I think how fast the days pass by sometimes I get blue,

But I'll have memories carry on what I can't keep of you.

I was living alone - I was on my own when I ran into an old friend,

Last time we talked... I don't know,

It had been since god knows when,

We used to be so close, used to share our clothes,

Hell, we shared a youth gone by,

Ten years later after brief small talk

We shared another goodbye.

Some summer songs are sung while sitting in the shade of an old oak tree,

Some summer songs go all night long to a youth who live carefree,

Sometimes sitting here I begin thinking bout all we used to be,

And though I have not sat here long,

I'm glad you're sitting with me.

Sunny time funny time laughing with my buddies while we share a bowl or two,

Start walking round talking about sweet little ventures and all we used to do,

Sometimes summertime passes by and brings on winter time blues,

But I'll have memories carry on what I can't keep of you.

Yes I'll have memories carry on what I can't keep of you.

CHAPTER THIRTY-THREE

RAT RACE

At the four o'clock hour

The rats come pouring from their dumpsters

Pouring into the city streets

Where they scream at each other

With horns built by others

Who understand

That the value of impatience

Sells itself to those in a hurry to go nowhere.

All of them rushing

To return to their lairs and rest

All of them tired

From the collective exhaustion

Of sitting on their asses all day

Mentally fatigued

From the screaming of the larger rats

Screaming that they did not accomplish enough of nothing

Or record enough nothing accomplished on paper

As these rats stream the streets

They carry with them

Backpacks, handbags, briefcases, man purses and laptops

All of them filled with the garbage

They collected all day in the dumpster but

Could not consume in one ass sitting

They will take them home

And hold them high above their nests

Filled with self-righteous pride

Over what it took to be a provider

And yes some self-pity

For how long it took them to carry their garbage home.

CHAPTER THIRTY-FOUR

OLD STONE ROWS

"In the field behind the church,

They've got these old stone rows,

And there are lots of flowers there,

But you won't find one that grows,

And there are hopes and dreams and cares,

But there are none you'll ever know,

They're buried neath the old stone rows,

They're buried neath the old stone rows."

"In the house up on the hill,

There lives a man who says he knows,

When people pass away,

Where it is that their souls go,

And he's never laid beside someone,

He's always lived alone,

He tends the spaces tween the old stone rows,

Says he knows where all the passing souls go."

"In the early morning hours,

There walks a lonely widowed soul,

She spent a lifetime living for someone,

now she walks on alone,

She hopes there is a life after,

The only life she'll ever know,

She prays for hope and mercy,

To the god who made her so,

And as her lonely life unfolds,

She walks the spaces tween the old stone rows.

She waits her place among the old stone rows.

We might think we choose our paths,

Determine all of our own roads,

As if the choices that we make

Determine where we go,

There's never any question when the answer we all know,

We all end up beneath the stone rows,

All paths end at the same cold road.

CHAPTER THIRTY-FIVE

NESTLED ARMS

(For Jaybee 1994)

Where within your nestled arms,

Do lie the Sacred beads and charms,

With which you conjure up sweet mists,

To tempt me so?

For there within your coal black eyes,

There hints of yet one more surprise,

Of stairs that but abruptly rise,

Beyond my sight.

Like candles in the night they glow,

Ever towards me - ever slow,

Yet with sufficient light with which,

To captivate my soul.

And now there lies but one more question,

Upon my lips - before unmentioned,

Out it seeps, when you look round,

Do you see me so?

CHAPTER THIRTY-SIX

ONLY ONE

Folk Melody

She's not the only girl that I have looked for,

She's just the only one,

Who offers so much more than one night stands,

Empty Clutching Hands,

She cannot understand why I love her,

Can she possibly, be so damn naive,

I mean I cannot see,

What she sees in me.

Living alone isn't always what it's supposed to be,

The American dream the bachelor scene,

No longer appeals to me,

She said...

I don't know but I love you so, please don't cheat on me,

I don't know but I love you so, please don't cheat on me.

She has everything that I have ever dreamed,

Dark brown eyes, a great big smile there to comfort me,

And all I know before I go to sleep,

My insecurities, have left me,

Living alone isn't always what it's supposed to be,

The American dream the bachelor scene,

No longer appeals to me,

She said...

I don't know but I love you so, please don't cheat on me,

I don't know but I love you so, please don't cheat on me.

CHAPTER THIRTY-SEVEN

IRISH BLESSING

A Folk medley =

Peace be with you where you go,

Peace be with you where you go,

Peace be with you where you go,

No matter how far, fast or slow.

May the sun shine down and light your way,

May the sun shine down and light your way,

May the sun shine down and light your way,

So you will return and stay.

May the path unfold before your feet,

May the path unfold before your feet,

May the path unfold before your feet,

Till your journey is complete,

Till your journey is complete,

Till you return home to me.

CHAPTER THIRTY-EIGHT

IN MY DAY

Bulletproof backpacks on converse dressed kids,

When I was your age!

We didn't have such things,

Turns my Frank Zappa poster smile upside down,

Makes me feel alone in my years,

Seeing your tears.

Synthetic drugs in the lungs block the voices of youth,

When I was your age!

We ate better snacks,

Far be it from me to tell you what to do,

But I feel bad just the same,

Feel bad for you.

Six figure schoolbooks carried by cross country kids,

Back in my day!

Well, we partied at school,

took summers off,

We only worked when we needed to,

I'm sorry you can't afford the school you go to,

I had no business criticizing and such.

Hoist the profit sails on the margin ships!

Your future's been floated down revenue streams,

When I was your age!

I lived both of our youths,

Now I am old and dependent on you,

What will I do?

CHAPTER THIRTY-NINE

A DAUGHTER'S JOURNEY

She holds hope in the thought,

That this boy might just save her,

From thoughts she has when alone,

She has fear that her thoughts,

If let out could betray her,

And turn to feelings inside,

She knows in her head,

that feelings can hurt her,

Just plain Thoughts are much safer Instead,

The love she has guides her and keeps her on course,

Through the forest of doubt in her soul,

When she falls and she fractures in so many pieces

As she mends she becomes truly whole.

CHAPTER FORTY

GYPSY DANCER

A gypsy girl with the beautiful barefoot blues,

Unafraid of the dark when the moon shines through,

Dancing and spinning her image to heart,

Like an overcast day that's filled with good news,

The road that she walks goes from rags to more ragged,

And the seams of her skirt go from torn to in tatters,

A grin curls soft lips because none of that matters,

Today she's the queen of the field.

CHAPTER FORTY-ONE

OH SMALL SAPLING

Oh small sapling,

Look how you have grown,

Through all the winter rages,

Over you've not blown,

And though I'm sure,

Your roots have thickened,

There's still much you do not know,

And look I see it pains you,

To hear me tell you so,

But one day you will be,

Old like me,

Your bark will harden chip away,

The wind will set it free,

And float it down the river,

Till it cannot be seen,

Do not fear - your times not here,

There's still much for you to see,

Before I pass away and lay,

Hidden among the leaves,

I pass to you a sacred rite,

A responsibility,

You must one day teach a sapling,

That it must one day be a tree.

CHAPTER FORTY-TWO

THE GOODBYE KISS

The goodbye kiss, so over valued,
Hangs upon our lips like a final apology
for all of the morning's mistreatments.
The necessity of the gesture easily avoided,
had there only been more loving hugs.

The silent unreturned longing glance,
It crosses the space between us,
It speaks to the things left unsaid,
Which would make peace if thoughts we're
expressed in words,
more eloquently than the anger we spoke
instead.

The long day spent apart,
Let's us pretend that healing is born of
not speaking.
Peace comes from distance.

By not being together we've mended our
ways,
Makes one think that the void is a healthy
place
that empty and without must be good.

The past that never returns,
Holds the truth to what once made us feel
close,
We are taught we must never look back,
Like an hourglass shifting from joyful
to sad,
It's only a matter of time,
Then we'll see if the past we refuse to
explore,
Holds the weight of more good times
or bad.

CHAPTER FORTY-THREE

THIS QUARENTINE AND ME

A thought dedicated to Langston Hughes and Ahmaud Arbery

If I could I would remain quarantined with you,

High up in our apartment above the city streets,

Safe from the virus for now but safe from other things as well,

Safe and far away from the stares of suspicion that judge us without hearing our words to know us,

Safe from the bullets that fly Both from the guns of the perps and the guns of the self righteous,

Safe from the intercom that calls security check when I walk down the aisle of a store,

Safe from the ads that run through my mind telling me to purchase more,

No... I'll remain here with you high up in our nest,

With a Birdseye view of what we are escaping,

Is it wrong that a virus has been good to me,

Is it wrong that it takes a pandemic quarantine to make me feel free?

CHAPTER FORTY-FOUR

HUNG UP

Sometimes I'm the shirt that's missing buttons that still hangs upon the pole next to other useful garments in your wardrobe.

I'm still the favorite piece of fabric that's most familiar to your form,

but now my purpose is to bring back memories fine but seldom thought of,

When your happiness decided for you what you wore.

My colors slightly faded,

It's not quite as bold and vibrant as that day so long ago,

when you first picked me from the store.

I miss and long for bygone days,

when I made you smile as you paused upon you way to check the mirror,

you'd look at me content as I would cling to you.

I was never going to be your Sunday best,

Those garments do not care a bit about how you feel,

only how others see you together.

While I wait patiently at home for that perfect rainy day when we're alone.

CHAPTER FORTY-FIVE

IT'S GONNA BE OKAY

You are the reason, the reason I'm okay,

You are the perfect ending to my shitty day,

You're the light that breaks through clouds and saves our outdoor play,

When you come round the sun comes out and keeps the storms at bay,

You are the reason. The reason I'm okay,

It's gonna be okay,

It's gonna be okay,

It's gonna be okay,

We're gonna be okay,

You are the reason, the reason I'm okay,

You're the sound that plays out loud when I've lost my way,

You're the lovely thoughts I have when I fall asleep,

You're the heads up penny found at random on the street,

You are the reason, the reason I'm okay,

It's gonna be okay,

Its gonna be okay,

It's gonna be okay,

We'll be okay,

There's not a minute passes in my day I don't hold dear,

No matter what that day brings down or if the outcome is not clear,

No matter how I struggle all day long against opposing views,

I just have to make it through the day then it's home and here with you,

Home and here with you,

Home and here with you,

Home and here with you,

I want to be with you,

You are the reason, the reason I'm okay,

You are a warm dry towel on a cold wet day,

You make the sky look brighter through the cloudy gray,

You can make the world seem right when you turn your smile my way,

Turn your smile my way,

It's gonna be okay

It's gonna be okay,

It's gonna be okay,

We're gonna be okay,

CHAPTER FORTY-SIX

ARE YOU OKAY?

You alright? You okay?

Seems like forever since we talked about nothing,

Seems like longer since we discussed things of real consequence.

I mean we're all Poli-Sci majors in this election year right?

Guess that means I'm not going to get that tart dough recipe I loved so much when last I really saw you.

No the grave concerns of America's foreign policy must outweigh the need to pleasure each other's souls with food.

I probably won't ever find out the words that go to the song that guided you through that rough patch,

I miss your conversational lectures on the importance of lyrics and your deep held convictions that the best musicians are poets,

That pales in importance to trade deals on the international stage though.

Are you alright? Are you okay?

Remember that time we met at the bridge and traded stories from high school like we could go back there?

We talked about how easy it was to fall in love,

When love didn't cost more than dinner and a movie.

You even caught me up on where some of those loves are now,

and we laughed then trailed off thinking about maybe it was what they ate,

or what movies they saw that led them to lives together,

Couldn't happen now.

We don't meet at a bridge but look across one,

There's too many conspiracies and I might be one of them,

on a different side than you in the new world order.

It's a shame really,

I liked cut watermelon before the concerts while hippie watching more than I like my opinions on healthcare,

I felt more complete calling ten points on girls with armpit hair than I do knowing I'm right about trade embargoes.

What was the moment this happened to us?

Are you alright? Are you okay?

I'm not.

CHAPTER FORTY-SEVEN

THE CROSSING

I will build for you this bridge over the river apathy,

Allowing us to cross safely.

I'm motivated to do so by my love for you.

It's been many days and nights in this place with you,

Where fear governs each waking moment,

Anticipating the fall of an angry gavel.

In this land where hope is a weakness and empathy is absent,

I'll hold your hand,

As I did when we crossed the river disparity with its wide churning waters,

Those waters threatened to pull us under like a warm comfortable drug,

Waters that we once gazed at for hours,

Lost in thoughts that seemed worth having but now seem to betray a purpose,

Undecided they sit still and conflicted,

Behind us the wall of ominous clouds threatening to drench us in the same water that lurks below,

Each drop would hit like a needle upon the skin,

Before it rolled like tears from the bridge to the river below,

Ahead lies an unknown shore hidden in a soft fog embankment,

It refuses to promise expectations to the presently hopeless who cross,

We will need to determine ourselves who we will be when we get there,

How we feel and what we will say about these times,

We will need to forget them.

I will build for you this bridge over the river apathy and together we will leave this place.

CHAPTER FORTY-EIGHT

THE SNOWGLOBE

I could spend a long time in one spot,

Silent, still, and unmoving,

Listening to the sound you make tuning your guitar,

And if it is in tune or if it's not,

Holds no special consequence for me,

I am hopelessly in love with each sound you bring.

I will barely breath

So as not to disturb the picture painting itself before me

As sunlight breaks from your hair which spills like water over your shoulder,

You stare intently at the neck of your guitar,

Almost as intently as I stare at you.

I would never leave this place,

There's nothing I want or need need beyond this moment shared with you,

The artist's brushstroke can end with a stunned smile upon my face,

As I sit for all eternity,

Here in this silent snow globe of chance making,

in continuum with you.

CHAPTER FORTY-NINE

WEATHERED & WORN

Painted glass pieces, are broken glass things,

Screen doors still slam with their mesh armor torn,

Raindrops can fall on a planned summer day,

But blue skies emerge when the storm clouds give way,

Lifetime's pass by in suburban brick homes,

Ticking clocks move the same speed when alone,

Freezing winds they can blow on a cold winter's day,

But flowers emerge after snows melt away.

CHAPTER FIFTY

Wherein lies the truth,

About how we feel today,

Wherein lies the truth,

On why we left that way,

Why'd we go on hurtful paths,

From roads of love we strayed,

Why is it easier to hurt,

With words we speak and say?

I want to scream out loud - words I
cannot say,

I want to shout, and hurt, and heal, and
stay,

I want to find the road that leads to where
we were,

I want to love again I want to feel okay,

Wherein lies the thought behind what we
say and do,

Wherein lies the truth behind the mask
on you,

What has happened to the simple value
of the truth,

What has happened to the girl I thought
I knew,

I want to scream out loud - words I
cannot say,

I want to shout, and hurt, and heal, and stay,

I want to find the road that leads to where
we were,

I want to love again I want to feel okay,

It's easier to run and hide - easier to flee,

It's sometimes tempting to act cowardly,

It's easier to walk away and think that
distance offers peace,

It's easier to turn inside of me,

I want to scream out loud - words I
cannot say,

I want to shout, and hurt, and heal, and stay,

I want to find the road that leads to where
we were,

I want to love again I want to feel okay,

I want to scream out loud - words I
cannot say,

I want to shout, and hurt, and heal, and stay,

I want to find the road that leads to where
we were,

I want to love again I want to feel okay."

CHAPTER FIFTY-ONE

TRAVEL SLOW

We us people should travel slow,

Just like leaves in water flow,

Uncaring where streams choose to go,

Content to ride along,

Often at night before I retire,

i sit upon hearth and poke at the fire,

Insisting its flames should dance much higher,

till the heat drives me away,

I'm not sure but I believe,

thank all things are as they must be,

this statement should also apply to me,

And I should be content.

Silly of me to assume,

That I like the breeze that blows in June,

Should test the leaves not yet to move,

They sit so patiently waiting.

CHAPTER FIFTY-TWO

EMILY'S ROOM

She washes the walls,

With her markers and pens,

Cleansing them of their prior empty indifference,

Each stroke, snippet or comment,

Cleaning the white nakedness which existed prior -

only to provide the potential to become dirty,

Now there exists something greater than not or don't do,

Something more than white nothing coating walls,

She's given the inside of her square,

A moment to speak out loud,

A voice which will serve to remind us,

Who once lived in there,

Must have been far too proud,

To shut up and simply lay down.

CHAPTER FIFTY-THREE

HOW WAS YOUR DAY

A song in the key of punk...

I wake up, and I look, at the day ahead,

I wake up, and I look, oh how my night was spent,

I head out, with the blues, just like I lost a friend,

I head out, and I think, I'm not going back again,

All I ever wanted was a woman who lived outside the lines of social conformity,

All I ever had was a two bit hag who folded napkins at home in conformist normalcy,

All I ever wanted was a woman content to live outside the wall of constructed subserviency,

All I ever had was a two bit hag who made the sign of the cross content with poverty,

I come home, and I think, oh how my life is lived,

I come home, and I wish, I had one more to live

I look up, at the walls. oh so paper thin,

I freak out, at the thought, I wish they'd all crash in,

All I ever wanted was a woman who lived outside the lines of content complacency

And all I ever had was a two bit hag who painted inside the box of social conformity

All I ever wanted was a woman content to question the rule of established authority,

All I ever had was a two bit hag content to live her life while moaning in misery,

I go out, and I turn, and run back in again,

I miss out, hanging round, with my family and friends,

I look out, peep the blinds, of my castle hall,

I freak out, safe inside, my own prison walls,

All I ever wanted was a woman who lived outside the lines of emerging theocracy

All I ever had was a two bit hag who counted prayers on beads in complete subserviency

All I ever wanted was a woman who lived life free from the chains of corporate marketing schemes

All I ever had was a two bit hag who purchased all of her rags in commercial subserviency.

CHAPTER FIFTY-FOUR

THE LONG WALK

The long walk home at the late night hour,

Seemed like a plausible thing

When decisions were made in daylight hours.

Staying a little longer always seemed the wiser,

When fun was being had at no one's expense.

A heavy weight of silence we carried,

Around long curving snake like streets,

The glow from high up street lights that caused shadows to creep from beneath our feet,

Words would have seemed ill advised in such silence,

They wouldn't have conveyed what the stillness spoke,

They would have only served to still the un-needed fears,

That walking at nighttime bring.

CHAPTER FIFTY-FIVE

SHADOW & LIGHT

For Jolie...

"Lost in a maze between shadow and light,

Too young for cares between wrong and right,

Too little to worry about which side I'm on,

Too lost in the art of my everyday life,

No time for anguish over internet news,

No cares for anger or political views,

Lost in the spacing between shadow and light,

I marvel at magic people miss in plain sight.

CHAPTER FIFTY-SIX

THE MANNEQUIN

"The art mannequin existed alone on the young girls shelf, till drawn in the lines of her pencils and pens. Though all alone, when her music played – he danced with the shadow partner in his mind."

LONELY SHADOW

A shadow left back when the body has gone,

It forgot to follow where it's master went,

Now it's bullied and pushed by the lamp top shades,

Till it cowers in corners of rooms.

BUS STOP

I don't even know your name,

Still I'm glad you came,

To the stop where we await the bus,

Due here in short time,

You know it certainly does me good,

To sit here in the morning sun,

And see this day has just begun,

With beauty like you who sits there to be seen.

Well now imagine if one day we should say,

Two paths just happens to cross that way,

A junction at which the two roads met,

And continued to go one way?

I see that you now rise to leave,

Imagine that I can't believe,

I'm all of a full four minutes time,

I never chanced to speak my mind,

My thoughts it seems we're only mine,

And I still don't know your name.

CHAPTER FIFTY-NINE

FORTRESS

Well now...

I've got a fortress where I hide,

And I don't let anyone else inside,

For fear of loosing my dignity,

For fear of loosing my pride,

And though the ice is slowly melting,

Down the thick stone tower walls,

Inside the seasons never changed,

Until you came along.

Well now...

I've got a fortress where I hide,

And I don't let anyone else inside,

For fear of loosing my dignity,

For fear of loosing my pride,

And though the ice is slowly melting,

Down the thick stone tower walls,

Inside the seasons never changed,

Until you came along.